It was pocket money day.
Rocky was going to the shop to spend his pocket money.

He saw Jamila in Wellington Square.

'What could I spend my money on, Jamila?' he said.
'You could spend it on a cap,' said Jamila.
'I have got a cap,' said Rocky.

They saw Kevin and Tony.

'You could get a ball,' said Kevin.
'I have got a ball,' said Rocky.

They went into the shop and Rocky looked for the money in his pocket.
It was not there!

'There is a hole in my pocket,' he said.
'My pocket money dropped out!'
They all looked for the money.

Fred went into the shop.
'There is a hole in his pocket,' said Jamila.
Fred laughed.

'His pocket money dropped out of the hole,' said Kevin.
Fred laughed again.

'Look,' he said, 'I have the money. It dropped out of his pocket in Wellington Square.'

They all laughed.
Rocky laughed too!

'I will spend it on cake for Fred and my friends!' said Rocky.